How to Analyze People: 2 Books in 1

-

Guide to Reading Anyone with Psychology Techniques, Including Dark Psychology and Manipulation

How to Analyze People:

The Ultimate Guide to Understand Body Language, Influence Human Behavior, Read Anyone with Proven Psychology Techniques

Dark Psychology:

How to Protect Yourself from Manipulation Techniques and Dark Psychology, Recognize and Control Emotional Manipulation

Table of Contents

How to Analyze People:

Dark Psychology:

How to Analyze People

The Ultimate Guide to Understand Body Language, Influence Human Behavior, Read Anyone with Proven Psychology Techniques

Introduction

You probably have noticed that most people don't often say what is on their mind. Most people say "Fine" or "okay" when they mean the opposite. There times that when you try to guess whether you should believe someone who tells you that they will think about it. This is particularly the case when you are onè field where finding out what is going on in a person's mind can determine how successful you will be.

All these will assist you in understanding what is going on in a person's mind, and this book will assist you to do just that.

This book will not give you some power to be a mind reader. What it will do is give you tools and tips so you can read the behavior and find out what most people think.

The truth is that you have been doing it for some time - when you have a feeling that you are attracted to someone or when you have a feeling that the person you are talking to is misleading or lying to you. By doing this, you have been unconsciously reading or analyzing people and their body language.

In this book, you will be able to learn about personality types and their traits. You will get to understand what you are made of and which category of personality type you fall into and others. If you really believe that you are perceptive or intuitive, when it comes to judging others, it means that you can analyze non-verbal cues well.

Most people don't exhibit their feelings. As a result, when you observe their behavior and actions correctly, it will allow you to have an insight into those emotions without really having a conversation with them

You can read universal behaviors, regardless of race, language, or race of the person that you want to observe. For you to be able to understand those behaviors well, you require to understand what the person is trying to represent. In this book, you will have a deeper understanding of that.

Chapter 1: Interpreting Body Language

Stare at the Face

Although many people control their facial expressions, you can be able to pick up on some nonverbal cues that you need to pay close attention.

Pay Close Attention, Particularly to the Mouth

A smile is a body attraction technique that can be used as a powerful gesture. Making a simple smile is a vital nonverbal cue that you have to pay attention to. There are two types of smiles—the fake smile and the sincere smile. A sincere smile suggests that the person you are interacting with is happy, and he/she is enjoying your company. On the contrary, a fake smile is used to suggest pleasure or approval, but it shows that the person making the fake smile is really feeling something totally different.

A half-smile is also a familiar facial expression that only involves one side of the mouth and it suggests uncertainty or sarcasm.

A slight grimace that lasts less than a second before a person makes a smile indicates that the person is trying to hide dissatisfaction behind the fake smile.

You may also notice a person's pursed, tight lips that may suggest displeasure, while a relaxed mouth suggests a positive mood and relaxed attitude.

When someone tries to cover their mouth or touch their lips when speaking, it should indicate to you that the person is lying.

Focus in the Eyes

Eye behavior is quite telling. When you are interacting with a person, you should pay close attention to whether the person is looking away or making direct eye contact. The inability for them to make direct eye contact can suggest they are not interested; they are secretive or bored. On the other hand, when the person looks down, it often suggests submissiveness or nervousness.

You should also pay attention to pupil dilation; this will determine whether the person is reacting favorably towards you. Naturally, pupils dilate when cognitive effort rate increases, so when someone is concentrating on you or something that they like, their pupils will definitely dilate. You should know that pupil dilation can be very challenging to detect, but under the perfect state, you should be able to notice.

The blinking rate of a person also indicates a lot of what a person is thinking internally. When a person is stressed and thinking a lot, the person will tend to blink at a higher rate. In some cases, increased blinking rate suggests that a person is lying, particularly when it is accompanied by touching the face.

You should also know that glancing at something so much is an expression. When a person is glancing at something so much, it indicates a desire for that thing. So when someone is glancing at the door during an interaction, you should know that the person desires to leave.

Mirroring

Mirroring includes mimicking another person's body expression. When you are engaging someone, you should check and see if the person mirrors your body language. For example, a mirroring gesture involves taking a sip of tea at the same time. When someone mimics your body expression, it is a good sign that he/she is creating a rapport.

Pay Attention to Someone's Feet

The feet are a part that people usually leak very vital nonverbal cues. The reason as to why many people unintentionally communicate nonverbal information via their feet is that they are often concentrating on their facial expression forgetting important clues are revealed through their feet. When sitting or standing, someone will direct their feet to the direction that they desire to go. When you notice that a person's feet are pointing to your direction, it is a good indicator that the person has a favorable view of you.

Observe the Movement of the Head

The rate at which a person nods their head when you are interacting with them suggests their patience or lack of it. You should notice that slow pace nodding suggests that the person is more interested in what you are discussing and desires that you continue talking. Fast pace nodding suggests that the person has heard enough of you and desires that you finish talking and give him/her time to talk.

Tilting of the head in a sideways manner is a sign of interest. Tilting your head backward during an interaction can be an indicator of uncertainty or suspicion.

Examine the Arms Position

You should think of the arms as the doorway to the self and the body. If someone crosses their arms while you interact with them, it is often suggested as a defensive expression. Crossing arms can again suggest a closed mind, anxiety, or vulnerability. You should also know that a crossed arm that is accompanied with a sincere smile and a generally relaxed posture, then this can suggest a confident, relaxed attitude. If a person places their arms on their hips, it suggests dominance and is more often used by men than women.

Nose Rubs

This expression is often associated with deception, and when you see a person rubbing his/her nose frequently, you should seriously consider that the person is not telling the entire truth.

Showing off the Neck

This is an expression that is mostly associated with women. When a woman extends her neck and shows it off to you, she is indicating that she is attracted to you. The neck is the most vulnerable part of her body, and she is entrusting it to you.

Chapter 2: Interpreting Verbal Communication

Open Communication

In most interpersonal interactions, the first few seconds are very vital. Your first impressions have a great impact on the success of future and further verbal communication with another person. When you first meet a person, you create an immediate impression of them; this is based on how they behave, sound, and look, as well as anything else you may have heard about them.

For example, when you meet a person and hear them speak, you create a judgment about their level of understanding and ability and their background. When you hear a foreign accent, for example, you might decide that you require to use simpler language for communication. You might realize that you need to listen more attentively to make sure that you understand what the person is saying.

Effective Verbal Communication

Effective speaking includes three main stages, that is, words that you choose to use, how you utter the words, and how you reinforce the words. All these areas have an impact on the transmission of your message and how the message is received and understood by the target audience.

It will be important for you to wisely and carefully choose the words to use. You will need to use different words in different events; even you are discussing a similar topic.

How you speak will include your pace and tone of voice. The pace and tone of voice communicate a certain message to the audience, for example, about your level of commitment and interest, or whether you are nervous about the audience reaction.

Active Listening

Effective listening is important for effective verbal communication. Ways that you can ensure that you listen more. These include:

- Be prepared to listen. Focus on the person speaking and not how you are going to reply to them
- Keeping an open mind while you avoid being judgmental about the person speaking.
- Always be objective
- Always focus on the objectivity of the message being conveyed
- Avoid distractions.
- Don't stereotype the person who's speaking.

Enhancing Verbal Communication

Techniques and tools that you can make use of to enhance the effectiveness of your verbal communication. These include:

- **_Reinforcement_**. It is used to encourage words alongside nonverbal clues, for example, a warm facial expression, head nods, and maintaining eye contact. All these assists in creating rapport and are likely to instill openness in others.

  Use of positive reinforcement and encouragement can:
  - Give assurance and allay fears
  - Show close interest in what others have to say
  - Maintain a close relationship and give way for the development
  - Show openness and warmth
  - Reduce nervousness or shyness in others and yourself

- **_Clarifying and Reflecting_**. It is a process involving giving feedback to another person of your understanding of what has been conveyed or said.

  Reflecting usually involves paraphrasing the message that has been conveyed to you by the speaker in your own words. All that you need to do is to capture the importance of the feelings and facts

13

expressed, and communicate your understanding back to the speaker.

Reflecting is an important skill because:

☐ You are demonstrating that you consider the other person's opinions

☐ The speaker received feedback about how the message has been received

☐ Shows respect for, and interest in, what the other person has to say

☐ You can view what you might have understood the message properly

- ***Questioning***. This is how broad we get more information from others on particular topics. It's an important way of clarifying aspects that are not clear or test your understanding. Questioning enables you to seek support from other people explicitly.

    Questioning is a vital technique because it helps you to draw another person into a conversation or simply to show interest.

Types of Questions

☐ Open question. These types of questions demand further elaboration and discussion. They help to broaden the scope of reply or response. These types of questions often take long to reply but give the other person a broader scope for encouraging and self-expression involvement in the interaction.

☐   Closed question. They seek only two or one-word answer, often simply 'no' or 'yes.' They allow the person asking the questions to be in total control of the interaction.

Chapter 3: Personality Type

How to Understand Personality Types

Realizing that areas of your personalities are engaged at different levels daily at work, home and play - is one thing, and understanding how to use that knowledge is another. But it is very vital. When you can identify personality types, it can assist you to exert your influence, enhance relationships, communicate effectively, and accomplish success in whatever desire is in play.

In this section, you will understand the different personality types and their building blocks, and you will realize that the personality type traits are what makes us all the same and at the same time it makes you different from the rest. Ensure that at the end of the study, you figure out where you lie in the sixteen personality types.

Personality type is defined as the psychological categorization of the various kinds of individuals. Personality types are sometimes separated from personality traits; the latter embodies a less categorization of behavioral tendencies. Personality types are also said to engage qualitative differences among people, while traits might be construed as quantitative differences.

ISTJ Personality - The Inspector

At your first impression, ISTJs are so intimidating. ISTJs are seen as formal, proper, and serious. ISTJs like old-school traits and traditions that uphold cultural responsibility, honor, patience, and hard work. ISTJs are upright, calm, and quiet.

I - Introvert: Self-sufficient, quiet, and reserved. Their energy is drained by them socializing. So they tend to be comfortable when they are alone. They process their thoughts internally. They need time to be alone for them to recharge.

S - Sensing: They are aware of, trust facts, details, specifics, present realities, and past experiences. ISTJs are often pragmatic, observant, and realistic. They live in the now-and-here.

T - Thinking: ISTJs make decisions mainly based on logic rather than their emotional feels. They are governed by their head and not their heart. They are very concerned with truths or facts than protecting other people's emotions.

J - Judging: They are disciplined, organized, and strategic. ISTJs are very responsible, and they stick to the schedules. They like to prepare and plan ahead.

ISTJs Traits

- They love to memorize facts and details
- ISTJs are people who are well respected in society
- They are calm and clear-headed during tense events
- They are committed and serious when it comes to relationships
- They are highly intelligent and have excellent planning skills
- ISTJs are mentally and physically organized
- They believe in traditions, and they tend to follow them to the latter.

INFJ Personality - The Counselor

These are idealists and visionaries who produce brilliant ideas and creative imaginations. INFJs have a totally different and very profound aspect of viewing the universe. Counselors tend to have a depth and substance in the manner they think, they never take anything at a surface level or accept things the way they are. Many people may perceive this kind of people as weird because they view life differently.

I - Introvert: Self-sufficient, quiet, and reserved. Their energy is drained by them socializing. So they tend to be comfortable when they are alone.

They process their thoughts internally. They need time to be alone to recharge.

N - Intuitive: Introspective, imaginative, and creative. They are perfect at analyzing complex topics. They mainly focus on the future rather than the present. They trust their gut instincts.

F - Feeling: INFJs tend to make use of their subjective criteria, values, and feeling when they are making decisions. They are mostly ruled by their hearts and not the head. They are very tactful, empathetic, and diplomatic. INFJs are mostly motivated by appreciation, and they prefer to avoid conflicts and arguments with others.

J - Judging: They are disciplined, organized, and strategic. INFJs are very responsible, and they stick to the schedules. They like to prepare and plan ahead.

INFJs Traits

- They are real visionaries who often try to make sense of life.
- They trust their gut instincts
- INFJs can understand and read other people easily
- They are cautious, courteous, helpful and sensitive
- Approachable, warm and caring
- They like creating and organizing systems

- INFJs are always passionate about dreams and ideas.

Creative and artistic, INFJs live in a world that has hidden possibilities and meanings. While INFJs place great value on order, they also are spontaneous; this is because INFJs intuitively understand things even without them being able to pinpoint why. It is because of this reason that INFJs are less orderly and systematic compared to the other judging personality type.

Intuition is one of the strongest values of the INFJs.

INFJs are very sensitive towards others feelings. They carefully do not hurt others through their actions and words. INFJs always lend a hand to others who need their assistance because they are empathizing and compassionate. They are good at sensing other's emotions and also good at analyzing people.

At the workplace, INFJs are very creative that makes them stand out from the crowd. They are strategists and planners who have respect for deadlines and rules.

INTJ Personality - The Mastermind

People in this personality type, as introverts, are reserved, comfortable, and quiet when they are alone. INTJs are normally self-sufficient, and they would prefer to work alone than in a group. INTJs live in a world full of strategy, analysis, and ideas.

I - Introvert: Self-sufficient, quiet, and reserved. Their energy is drained by them socializing. So they tend to be comfortable when they are alone. They process their thoughts internally. They need time to be alone to recharge.

N - Intuitive: Introspective, imaginative, and creative. They are perfect at analyzing complex topics. They mainly focus on the future rather than the present. They trust their gut instincts.

T - Thinking: INTJs make decisions mainly based on logic rather than their emotions. They are ruled by their head and not by their heart. They are very concerned with truths facts rather than protecting other people's emotions.

J - Judging: They are disciplined, organized, and strategic. INTJs are very responsible, and they stick to the schedules. They like to prepare and plan ahead.

INTJs Traits
- INTJs get bored with mundane routine duties, small talk, and surface level thinking.

- They are extremely logic, and they value efficiency and knowledge
- Have high standards for performance, which the INTJs apply to themselves more strongly.
- INTJs are very reserved and are detached from the rest, but they value close relationships.
- They can absorb very complex theoretical material
- INTJs are supreme strategists who are rational, future-oriented, and logical.
- They have strong intuition and insights; hence, they can see the bigger picture.

The core of an INTJ type is mainly formed by the thinking and intuitive traits; these traits make them open-minded, utilitarian individuals and more intelligent, having the capability of amazing intellectual feats. INTJs have fast and versatile minds that allow them to enjoy intellectual tasks, and they will feel bored when not intellectually motivated.

They are long-range thinkers, ambitious, deliberate, and self-confident. Typical types of personality find themselves in career choices that range from engineering and sciences.

A person of the INTJ personality type is very ruthless when it comes to analyzing the importance of ideas and methods. While other people accept the argument that things have been done in a particular way, you will find INTJs challenging and questioning the existing procedures. This makes INTJs very efficient and more impartial decision makers.

They will utter what they think and will give solutions that they believe are appropriate without them sugarcoating their words. They rely much on their mind rather than their heart and tend to safeguard or suppress their feelings.

They can care deeply for others, but only bestow that care to only a select few. INTJs are willing to spend most of their effort and time on an engagement that they consider to be worthwhile. INTJs prefer to develop a few important friendships rather than a large group of acquaintances. They are likely to be more positive, healthy relationships; this is because they are likely to abandon engagements that do not work for them. They believe in constant growth to the relationship. Their strongest interpersonal asset is their willingness and ability to work at a relationship.

ENFJ Personality - The Giver

These are focused on people. ENFJs are charismatic, outspoken, idealistic, extroverted, ethical, and highly principled, and they understand how to connect and interact with other people no matter their personality or background. They really rely on their feelings and intuition; they live a life full of imagination rather than in the actual world. Instead of the ENFJs concentrating on living in the "now" and want is happening currently, they tend to focus on the abstract and what could happen in the future possibly.

E - Extrovert: These kinds of people like to be around people. They have high energy levels and are very active. ENFJs like to take up the initiative. They are enthusiastic and outgoing. They tend to talk more than listen.

N - Intuitive: Introspective, imaginative, and creative. They are perfect at analyzing complex topics. They mainly focus on the future rather than the present. They trust their gut instincts.

F - Feeling: ENFJs tend to make use of their subjective criteria, values, and feeling when they are making decisions. They are mostly ruled by their hearts and not the head. They are very tactful, empathetic, and diplomatic. ENFJs are mostly motivated by appreciation, and they prefer to avoid conflicts and arguments with others.

J - Judging: They are disciplined, organized, and strategic. ENFJs are very responsible, and they stick to the schedules. They like to prepare and plan ahead.

ENFJs Traits

- They are good communicators
- They are very organized and effective with challenges when it comes to dealing with uncertainties
- ENFJs are very open-minded and highly accepting of others
- They are firm and passionate when it comes to principles and ideals.
- Generous, warm, focused and caring
- Highly reflective and intuitive
- Genuinely kind, influential, reliable, and loyal.

ISTP Personality - The Craftsman

These are very mysterious people who are normally logical and quite rational, but they are also enthusiastic and spontaneous. ISTPs often have the capability of humorously insightful observations about the universe around them. ISTPs traits are less easy to recognize than other personality types, even for those who know the traits very well cannot often anticipate their reactions. People with ISTP personality type, deep down they are unpredictable, spontaneous, but they tend to hide the traits from the outside world, often more successfully.

I - Introvert: Self-sufficient, quiet, and reserved. Their energy is drained by them socializing. So they tend to be comfortable when they are alone. They process their thoughts internally. They need time to be alone to recharge.

S - Sensing: They are aware of, trust facts, details, specifics, present realities, and past experiences. ISTPs are often pragmatic, observant, and realistic. They live in the now-and-here.

T - Thinking: ISTPs make decisions mainly based on logic rather than their emotions. They are ruled by their head and not by their heart. They are very concerned with truths facts rather than protecting other people's emotions.

P - Perceiving: Keeping options open, preferring spontaneity, and flexibility. ISTPs are very adaptive, and they go with the flow. They are playful and are less aware of the time. They prefer to begin a project, and they question the need for many rules.

ISTP Traits
- They are determined and independent
- ISTPs are more focused on living in the present rather than in the future
- They are normally laid back and are easygoing with most people
- ISTP is a risk taker who likes new and variety of experiences

- They are better troubleshooters who are easily able to get solutions to practical issues.
- ISTPs are result-oriented, highly practical and realistic
- They often put together facts about the environment and store them away for later use.

ISTPs are generous and optimistic; they believe that equality and fairness are vital. ISTPs have a strong drive to know well the way things work. They are perfect in logic analysis, are action-oriented, and they enjoy the practical application. ISTPs are adaptable, and they normally have good technical skills. They have a very compelling drive to understand the way things work.

ISTPs are usually easygoing with others and confident in their capabilities. Many people will describe ISTPs as friendly but quite calm, private but suddenly spontaneous, and very curious but not able to stay focused on formal studies.

Their decisions mainly stem from a sense of practical realism and a do unto others attitude. Equality and fairness are very vital to ISTPs. ISTPs are very loyal to their friends, but they may require a lot of time alone for them to recharge.

ISTP personality types are likely to be good at regulating the energy levels and saving the energy for things that they consider vital. This is particularly noticeable in events where ISTPs get an opportunity to work something they like, like a hobby project. The amount of energy and effort ISTPs they can expend in this kind of situations is very impressive.

ESFJ Personality - The Provider

A person with this type of personality is a stereotypical extrovert. ESFJs are like social butterflies; their urge to socialize with people and make them happy often ends up making the ESFJs very popular. ESFJs tend to be sports hero or cheerleaders in college or high school. This is a very common type of personality and one that is loved by many people.

E - Extrovert: These kinds of people like to be around people. They have high energy levels and are very active. ESFJs like to take up the initiative. They are enthusiastic and outgoing. They tend to talk more than listen.

S - Sensing: They are aware of, trust facts, details, specifics, present realities, and past experiences. ESFJs are often pragmatic, observant, and realistic. They live in the now-and-here.

F - Feeling: ESFJs tend to make use of their subjective criteria, values, and feeling when they are making decisions. They are mostly ruled by their hearts and not the head. They are very tactful, empathetic, and diplomatic. ESFJs are mostly motivated by appreciation, and they prefer to avoid conflicts and arguments with others.

J - Judging: They are disciplined, organized, and strategic. ESFJs are very responsible, and they stick to the schedules. They like to prepare and plan ahead.

ESFJ Traits
- ESFJs prefer to live in the real world rather than in their own imaginations.
- Empathetic and compassionate
- They really often ready to listen with sincere and warmth sensitivity
- Sociable, energetic, helpful and sensitive
- They are well-liked and popular
- ESFJs are real extroverts and social butterflies

INFP Personality - The Idealist
INFPs are quite reserved. INFPs prefer not to speak about themselves, particularly in their first interaction with a new person. INFPs love spending most of their time to be alone in a very quiet environment where they can make sense of what is going on around them. People with this kind of personality type like analyzing symbols and signs. They consider the symbols and signs of being metaphors that have deeper definitions that

are associated with life. INFPs, most of their time, are lost in their daydreams and imaginations; they are often drowned in the depth of their ideas, thoughts, and fantasies.

I - Introvert: Self-sufficient, quiet, and reserved. Their energy is drained by them socializing. So they tend to be comfortable when they are alone. They process their thoughts internally. They need time to be alone to recharge.

N - Intuitive: Introspective, imaginative, and creative. They are perfect at analyzing complex topics. They mainly focus on the future rather than the present. They trust their gut instincts.

F - Feeling: INFPs tend to make use of their subjective criteria, values, and feeling when they are making decisions. They are mostly ruled by their hearts and not the head. They are very tactful, empathetic, and diplomatic. INFPs are mostly motivated by appreciation, and they prefer to avoid conflicts and arguments with others.

P - Perceiving: Keeping options open, preferring spontaneity, and flexibility. INFPs are very adaptive, and they go with the flow. They are playful and are less aware of the time. They prefer to begin a project, and they question the need for many rules.

INFP Traits

- They avoid feuds and are good mediators
- They strive to make the universe a better place
- INFPs like being around people, they are naturally compassionate and warm
- They tend to avoid harming other people's emotions, but sometimes they can be very controlling
- They are highly prospective and intuitive: they are good at making others feel comfortable
- INFPs love life and all that comes with life
- They're fast and spontaneous to cope, but hard on themselves over perceived failures.

Their main goals are to serve humanity and to discover their life's definition. They are perfectionists and idealists who drive themselves hard to accomplish these goals. INFPs are very intuitive about others, and they depend heavily on their intuitions to guide them.

They are good listeners, thoughtful, and considerate who put others at ease. INFPs are reserved in expressing their own feelings but sincerely care about other people and wish to understand them. When caught up in conflict events, they will strive to understand both parties side of the argument and avoiding hurting emotions, no matter which party is right or wrong. While other people make decisions based on their past experiences, they depend heavily on their gut feelings and intuition. INFPs look beyond past experience to look for an underlying definition. INFPs find patterns and signs in daily situations and consider symbols and metaphors that they see around them when they make decisions.

They tend to have their own set of principles and standards from which INFPs base their decisions and actions. They tend to have a very strong personal value system. All their actions and words rely on whether or not they fit into that system. They have high standards that make them real perfectionists. They work and fight hard for whatever's on their plate, and no matter how simple the task may seem, it becomes their cause of action.

They are idealists who care very much about the world they live in. INFPs feel like their existence is to make the world a better place for every person. INFPs are existentialists; they are often seeking the purpose and definition of their lives.

ESFP Personality - The Performer

Performers have an observant, perceiving, feeling, and extroverted personality trait and they are often seen as good entertainers. They are born to be in front of other people and to capture the stage; this type loves the spotlight. They are persons with very strong interpersonal techniques. ESFPs are fun and lively, and they enjoy being the epitome of attention. ESFPs are sympathetic, generous, concerned, friendly, and warm towards other people's well-being.

E - Extrovert: These kinds of people like to be around people. They have high energy levels and are very active. ESFPs like to take up the initiative. They are enthusiastic and outgoing. They tend to talk more than listen.

S - Sensing: They are aware of, trust facts, details, specifics, present realities, and past experiences. ESFPs are often pragmatic, observant, and realistic. They live in the now-and-here.

F - Feeling: ESFPs tend to make use of their subjective criteria, values, and feeling when they are making decisions. They are mostly ruled by their hearts and not the head. They are very tactful, empathetic, and diplomatic. ESFJs are mostly motivated by appreciation, and they prefer to avoid conflicts and arguments with others.

P - Perceiving: Keeping options open, preferring spontaneity, and flexibility. ESFPs are very adaptive, and they go with the flow. They are playful and are less aware of the time. They prefer to begin a project, and they question the need for many rules.

ESFP Traits

- ESFPs have a very detailed approach to life and appreciation for the universe around them.
- They have the talent to entertain those around them.
- They have a practical aptitude for common sense
- ESFPs tend to live in the here-and-now and likes excitement
- They have a natural capability to understand the realities and facts of the world.
- They have very strong interpersonal skills, and they enjoy being the center of attention.
- Sympathetic, generous, warm, and concerned for others.

ENFP Personality - The Champion

The Champions have an intuitive, perceiving, feeling, and an extroverted personality. ENFPs are highly individualistic, and they tend to drive towards building their own habits, looks, ideas, actions, and methods - champions don't love cookie cutter individuals and hate when they are forced to live in a tiny box. ENFPs tend to be around people, and they have a very strong intuitive nature when it comes to others and themselves. ENFPs tend to operate from their emotions most of their time, and they are very thoughtful and perceptive.

E – Extrovert: These kinds of people like to be around people. They have high energy levels and are very active. ENFPs like to take up the initiative. They are enthusiastic and outgoing. They tend to talk more than listen.

N - Intuitive: Introspective, imaginative, and creative. They are perfect at analyzing complex topics. They mainly focus on the future rather than the present. They trust their gut instincts.

F - Feeling: ENFPs tend to make use of their subjective criteria, values, and feeling when they are making decisions. They are mostly ruled by their hearts and not the head. They are very tactful, empathetic, and diplomatic. ESFJs are mostly motivated by appreciation, and they prefer to avoid conflicts and arguments with others.

P - Perceiving: Keeping options open, preferring spontaneity, and flexibility. ENFPs are very adaptive, and they go with the flow. They are playful and are less aware of the time. They prefer to begin a project and question the need for many rules.

ENFP Traits

- They are focused and are future-oriented over short-term desires.
- They have a resistance to being ruled and directed by other people
- They often can grasp challenging theories and concepts with ease.
- They can relate and interact with others and feel and think as they do
- ENFPs dislike performing mundane, routine, or boring tasks.
- Sincere and warmly interested in other people
- They enjoy being around other people.

They are lucky in that they are perfect at various things. ENFPs can accomplish a perfect degree of achievement at anything they are interested in. However, they are bored easily and aren't naturally perfect at following things through to completion. ENFPs should avoid doing tasks that need performing a lot of routine-oriented, detailed tasks. ENFPs will perform well in professions that allow them to create new ideas and deal with others creatively. They tend not to be very happy in positions that are regimented and confining.

Compared to other extroverts, ENFPs require time to be alone to focus and ensure that they are in the direction that aligns with their values. Those that remain focused will often be very successful at their projects, as long as they follow them through till the end. They are naturally happy people unless they are restricted to strict mundane tasks or schedules. ENFPs that are not happy can misuse their gift, and they may end up being very manipulative due to their charm make it easy for them to achieve what they desire. Luckily, many of them do not misuse their natural capabilities. This is because they will be going against their natural personal values and principles.

Relationships are very central to this kind of people. They often are hands-on and are mostly engaged with their intimate relationships. ENFPs have the habit of asking their partners how they are faring. This habit may be smothering, but it supports a very strong awareness of the health of the relationship. They require to given positive affirmations and assurance. ENFPs like lavishing affection and love on their partners, and are energetic and creative in their efforts to please.

They are enthusiastic and warm individuals who are full of potential and very bright. They tend to live in a world full of opportunities and become excited and passionate about things. ENFPs enthusiastic nature provides them with the capability to motivate and inspire other people. ENFPs can talk their way out of anything and in anything. ENFPs see life as a very special gift, and they work hard to make the most out of it.

ESTP Personality - The Doer

The Doers are ruled by the need for emotions, social engagements and feelings, reasoning, and logical processing, along with a need for total freedom. Abstracts and theories do not keep them quite interested for a long time. People having this kind of personality type tend to leap before they look, mending their shortcomings as they go through, rather than preparing contingency plans or sitting idle.

E - Extrovert: These kinds of people like to be around people. They have high energy levels and are very active. ESTPs like to take up the initiative. They are enthusiastic and outgoing. They tend to talk more than listen.

S - Sensing: They are aware of, trust facts, details, specifics, present realities, and past experiences. ESTPs are often pragmatic, observant, and realistic. They live in the now-and-here.

T - Thinking: ESTPs make decisions mainly based on logic rather than their emotions. They are ruled by their head and not by their heart. They are very concerned with truths facts rather than protecting other people's emotions.

P - Perceiving: Keeping options open, preferring spontaneity, and flexibility. ESTPs are very adaptive, and they go with the flow. They are playful and are less aware of the time. They prefer to begin a project and question the need for many rules.

ESTP Traits

- They are attracted to risks and adventures.
- They tend to live in the present moment and like to see instant outcomes.
- Doers love to have fun and for them to be the center of attention.
- Doers are fast-talking and fast moving with an appreciation for the finer details of life.
- ESTPs have an uncanny capability to perceive people's motivations and attitudes
- Doers have a strong flair for style and drama

Their spontaneous approach to life makes a particular work environment, school, and other very organized situations difficult for them. This is not because they are not intelligent, but because Doers are opposed to highly regulated and structured environments.

At home, workplace, school, or at any social gathering, it is quite easy to spot Doers. Spontaneous and spirited, fun loving and even slightly crass, people with this kind of personality type are go-getters who tend to take on life head-on, and they love being engaged and active. They play hard and work hard, and they expect everyone to adopt the same mentality while they are around ESTPs. It is natural for ESTPs to have the ability for networking and to make new pals; this is because of their outgoing nature and their drive to be successful. These traits make it easier for them to get along very well with anybody they come across with, so long as they are not deemed flaky, complainers, lazy or liars.

When it comes to relationships, ESTPs are usually not described as being the type that sits and yearns away for their wedding day. Life is full of surprises and fun, and no greater happiness can be found than in living in the experience and moment all that life has offered, free of limitations and ties. ESTPs may not spend most of their time planning for their future, but their unpredictability and enthusiasm make them spontaneous and entertaining when dating their partners.

This personality type is certainly the party type. With an enviable invigorating and imagination sense of spontaneity, they are never boring as such. ESTPs like adventuring interesting ideas, both in discussion and by moving out and seeing it for themselves.

When it comes to career choices, the action is the word of the day. They are people who want to go out and be on the go, seeing, experiencing, and doing things. Doers prefer to be on the field rather than being stuck behind desks.

ESTJ Personality - The Supervisor

The supervisors are people who are traditional, dedicated, organized, dignified, honest, and they are great believers of performing what they believe is socially acceptable and good. Though the ways to right and good are challenging, ESTJs are happy to take their places as the rightful leaders of the group. ESTJs are the center and apex of good citizenry.

E - Extrovert: These kinds of people like to be around people. They have high energy levels and are very active. ESTJs like to take up the initiative. They are enthusiastic and outgoing. They tend to talk more than listen.

S - Sensing: They are aware of, trust facts, details, specifics, present realities, and past experiences. ESTJs are often pragmatic, observant, and realistic. They live in the now-and-here.

T - Thinking: ESTJs make decisions mainly based on logic rather than their emotions. They are ruled by their head and not by their heart. They are very concerned with truths facts rather than protecting other people's emotions.

J -Judging: They are disciplined, organized, and strategic. ESTJs are very responsible, and they stick to the schedules. They like to prepare and plan ahead.

ESTJ Traits

- Supervisors are responsible, and they would rather strategize and plan before they act.
- They concentrate on what is practical, preferring order and tradition
- They are very organized and have challenges in dealing with uncertainties
- They are great strategists and outstanding game player
- Supervisors are honest, hardworking, ethical and dedicated
- They are principled, dignified, and strong-willed
- ESTJs are very loyal to the group, whether it is a country, family, or community.

People look towards ESTJs for counsel and guidance, and they are always happy when they are asked for assistance. They like being role models and organizing events and bringing people together, particularly if the events call for upholding values and traditions.

ESTJs have the innate capability to make the most complex and challenging of tasks seem easy. Not only do supervisors love working towards a goal, but they are also very organized while they work towards the goal. They believe that manual labor and hard work build character.

Being extroverts, they do not like working alone. ESTJs like working with people and expects to them to be hardworking and dedicated as they are. This will lead to them reacting negatively whey they feel that the people around them are dishonest, lazy, or unreliable. They live in a world of truths - truths that can be experienced, felt, observed, and touched. ESTJs are very sure of what they believe and know in that anything that does not coincide with their principles and standards are considered unacceptable and wrong. When they are not able to tolerate unconventional and uncomfortable events, they may easily fall into the trap of them being judgmental. Anything different or new can be avail elf dress to them, and they would rather do things in a manner they have always done them. To them, comfort means reliability, and being forced out of their comfort zones means instability.

ENTJ Personality - The Commander

Their main purpose of life concentrates on external areas, and all their issues are dealt with logically and rationally. Their secondary purpose of the operation is more internal, where reasoning and intuition take center stage. They are naturally born leaders, and they like to be in charge. Commanders live in a world full of opportunities, and they usually view obstacles and difficulties as great opportunities for them to push ahead. This personality type seems to have a natural gift for making decisions, leadership, and considering ideas and options quickly yet with great care.

E - Extrovert: These kinds of people like to be around others. They have high energy levels and are very active. ENTJs like to take up the initiative. They are enthusiastic and outgoing. They tend to talk more than listen.

N - Intuitive: Introspective, imaginative, and creative. They are perfect at analyzing complex topics. They mainly focus on the future rather than the present. They trust their gut instincts.

T - Thinking: ENTJs make decisions mainly based on logic rather than their emotions. They are ruled by their head and not by their heart. They are very concerned with truths facts rather than protecting other people's emotions.

J - Judging: They are disciplined, organized, and strategic. ENTJs are very responsible, and they stick to the schedules. They like to prepare and plan ahead.

ENTJ Traits
- They have a great sense of self-confidence and are sure of themselves and their capabilities
- They can be perfectionists
- Commanders have well-developed communication techniques.

- They are project-oriented and tend to concentrate on the task at hand
- They have thoughtful and logical reasoning before they take any action.
- They are naturally born leaders, and they like to be in charge
- ENTJs tend to live in a world full of opportunities and possibilities

Something that an ENTJ enjoys the most is a good challenge, whether the challenge is small or big. They believe that there is no limit to what they can accomplish if they are given resources and ample time. These traits make them powerful business leaders and successful entrepreneurs. They push for their desire through the sheer will power and keep on pressing when almost everyone else would want them to surrender or have given up.

They have a growth-oriented approach when it comes to relationships, and they will seize any chance to enhance themselves. They expect logical thinking from their partners and friends; it is perplexing and surprising to them when people do not share this attitude on family, life, and love.

A combination of strong will, logical reasoning, and intelligence skills are a force to be reckoned with, ENTJs tend to fight tooth and nails get over whatever obstacle that may come their way. The fearsome intellect and determination allow them to get over many difficulties and to be successful in love, personal life, school, business, and professional life. They require to put ones conscious effort to help them enhance their weaker traits and build additional techniques that can complement their determination and their analytical habits and minds.

INTP Personality - The Thinker

Thinkers are known in your society and in daily life, their excellent theories and unrelenting logic that makes sense since INTPs are arguably the most logical mind of all personality types. INTPs love patterns, and they have a very keen eye for picking up on discrepancies, and a perfect capability to analyze people, making it not a good idea to lie to an INTP type person. These kinds of people are not interested in daily activities, but they find an environment where their creative potential and genius can be showcased, there is no time limit and energy they will spend in enhancing the unbiased and very insightful solution.

I - Introvert: Self-sufficient, quiet, and reserved. Their energy is drained by them socializing. So they tend to be comfortable when they are alone. They process their thoughts internally. They need time to be alone to recharge.

N - Intuitive: Introspective, imaginative, and creative. They are perfect at analyzing complex topics. They mainly focus on the future rather than the present. They trust their gut instincts.

T - Thinking: INTPs make decisions mainly based on logic rather than their emotions. They are ruled by their head and not by their heart. They are very concerned with truths facts rather than protecting other people's emotions.

P - Perceiving: Keeping options open, preferring spontaneity, and flexibility. INTPs are very adaptive, and they go with the flow. They are playful and are less aware of the time. They prefer to begin a project, and they question the need for many rules.

INTP Traits

- They are primarily easy-going and laid back
- INTPs love like new ideas and are more excited about new theories
- They are not very well equipped to face the emotional need of other people.
- They are usually original, independent and unconventional
- They have a high value of knowledge and intelligence

Due to their originality and unconventionality nature, they are likely not to place value on traditional desires such as security and popularity.

INTPs normally have very complex traits, and they may be temperamental and restless. Thinkers are very ingenious and may tend to have unconventional thought sequences that allow them to analyze ideas in new ways properly.

They live in a world full of theoretical opportunities. Thinkers view everything in terms of how it could be enhanced or what it could be turned into. Most scientific breakthroughs have been made to pass by INTPs. They are at best when they are allowed to work on their theories on their own without any interference.

Thinkers have a strong capability to analyze challenges, identify sequences, and come up with logical explanations. Just like INTJs, INTPs have great value for knowledge. They tend to approach theories and challenges with skepticism and enthusiasm, neglecting the existing opinions to define their own approach.

Thinkers don't like to control or lead people. They are flexible and tolerant in most events that occur, unless one of the strongly held beliefs has been challenged or violated, in that case, INTPs takes a rigid stance

They hold little or no value for decisions made on personal feelings or subjectivity. Thinkers strive to constantly accomplish logical conclusions to challenges. Due to this, they are normally not in-tune with how others feel and are not well equipped when it comes to meeting the emotional needs of other people.

ISFJ Personality - The Nurturer

The Nurturers are philanthropists; they are often are ready to give back and return generosity with more generosity. They are kind-hearted and warm. Nurturers have value for cooperation and peace and are likely to be more sensitive when it comes to other people's emotions and feelings. Many people have great value of the ISFJ personality type for their awareness and consideration and their capability to bring out the best in other people.

I - Introvert: Self-sufficient, quiet, and reserved. Their energy is drained by them socializing. So they tend to be comfortable when they are alone. They process their thoughts internally. They need time to be alone to recharge.

S - Sensing: They are aware of, trust facts, details, specifics, present realities, and past experiences. ISFJs are often pragmatic, observant, and realistic. They live in the now-and-here.

F - Feeling: ISFJs tend to make use of their subjective criteria, values, and feeling when they are making decisions. They are mostly ruled by their hearts and not the head. They are very tactful, empathetic, and diplomatic. ISFJs are mostly motivated by appreciation, and they prefer to avoid conflicts and arguments with others.

J - Judging: They are disciplined, organized, and strategic. ISFJs are very responsible, and they stick to the schedules. They like to prepare and plan ahead.

ISFJ Traits

- They can be relied on to follow a task through to its completion.
- They have joy in creating structures, and they value security
- Nurturers are very uncomfortable when it comes to confrontation and feuds.
- They are very dependable
- They do not like abstract thoughts and theories
- Down-to-earth, stable and more practical
- ISFJs are considerate and kind, and they are more aware of other people's emotions and feelings

They have a natural tendency to be hardworking and are usually meticulous to the point of perfectionism. They take a personal interest in responsibility for their obligations, work, and desire; consistently, they go above and beyond; they do everything they can to not just to meet but exceed all the expectations.

ENTP Personality - The Visionary

This is one of the rarest personality types in the universe; this is understandable. Even though the Visionaries are extroverts, ENTPs do not enjoy small talk, and they may not be successful in social interaction, particularly those that may involve people who are very different from the ENTP type. Visionaries are very knowledgeable and intelligent. They require constant motivation. ENTPs can discuss facts and theories in extensive detail. ENTPs are objective, rational, and logical when it comes to how they approach arguments and information

E - Extrovert: These kinds of people like to be around people. They have high energy levels and are very active. ENTPs like to take up the initiative. They are enthusiastic and outgoing. They tend to talk more than listen.

N - Intuitive: They are introspective, imaginative, and creative. They are perfect at analyzing complex topics. They mainly focus on the future rather than the present. They trust their gut instincts.

T - Thinking: ENTPs make decisions mainly based on logic rather than their emotions. They are ruled by their head and not by their heart. They are very concerned with truths facts rather than protecting other people's emotions.

P - Perceiving: Keeping options open, preferring spontaneity, and flexibility. ENTPs are very adaptive, and they go with the flow. They are playful and are less aware of the time. They prefer to begin a project and also question the need for many rules.

ENTP Traits

- Have good social techniques
- Highly knowledgeable and competent
- Ingenious in solving problems and highly innovative.
- They value freedom
- They do not like to be governed
- Charming, creative and smart
- They like to create theorize and ideas

They get great pleasure from interacting in intellectual interactions such as debates. They are not afraid to question anything they feel is not right, and they will tend to dismiss other people's ideas or thoughts if they can't be justified with logic and reason.

Visionaries are fast witted and humorous, but also they can sound condescending and arrogant. Even though they are sociable, they can also be detached from the rest. This makes them less receptive to others feelings; at times, they are referred to as inconsiderate and insensitive.

ISFP Personality - The Composer

The composers are introverts, but they do not seem like introverts. This is so because when they have challenges in connecting to others at first, they try to become friendly, approachable, and warm at the end. ISFPs are fun to be in your company and quite spontaneous, that makes them the appropriate pal to be within any activity, regardless of the activity is planned for or not. This kind of people always desire to live their personal life to the fullest and will always embrace the present, so that they ensure that they are often out to discover new experiences and challenges. It is from the experiences that they harness their wisdom, so they do see great value in interacting with new people than the other introverts.

I - Introvert: Self-sufficient, quiet, and reserved. Their energy is drained by them socializing. So they tend to be comfortable when they are alone. They process their thoughts internally. They need time to be alone to recharge.

S - Sensing: They are aware of, trust facts, details, specifics, present realities, and past experiences. ISFPs are often pragmatic, observant, and realistic. They live in the now-and-here.

F - Feeling: ISFPs tend to make use of their subjective criteria, values, and feeling when they are making decisions. They are mostly ruled by their hearts and not the head. They are very tactful, empathetic, and diplomatic. ISFPs are mostly motivated by appreciation, and they prefer to avoid conflicts and arguments with others.

P - Perceiving: Keeping options open, preferring spontaneity, and flexibility. ISFPs are very adaptive, and they go with the flow. They are playful and are less aware of the time. They prefer to begin a project and question the need for many rules.

ISFPs Traits
- They do not like restrictions
- They are always considerate of how others feel and tactful
- ISFPs love to try new experiences
- ISFPs are very disciplined internally, but they appear highly spontaneous externally
- They love adventure and are free-spirited
- They love figures and facts and not ideas and theories
- They do not like uncertainties in life, but they can easily adapt to change

Importance of Understanding Personality Types

- Helps you to know your preferences. Everyone has their personal psychological type choices, and operating within these choices typically allows you to be most effective, efficient, and your most comfortable self. Contrary, when you operate outside these limits, you will need to use more time and energy, which will result in low quality of work.

- Avoid conflicts. Recognizing and understanding your personality type can help you diffuse conflicts even before they arise.

- Finding an appropriate career. Your personality type plays a major role in whether you are suited in a particular profession, how good you perform your day-to-day tasks, and even your general job satisfaction.

- Appreciate diversity. Recognizing and understanding your personality type and how it differs from the rest and those you interact with. It gives you a great appreciation for diversity and what it adds to your company, work, environment, and team.

- Enhance decision-making capabilities. How you make decisions is mainly based on your intuition versus sensing preference. If you are a sensing individual, you are likely to feel out a situation before you make a choice.

Chapter 4: Spotting a Deceptive Behavior and Lies

What is Deception?

It refers to a cruel act of causing a person to believe something that is not true. You should know that even the most sincere people practice deception.

When the verbal aspect and the visual aspect of a message do not align, then you are doomed. Here are some tips that will show you when a person is telling a lie:

- Building rapport. Good cops normally get better outcomes compared to bad cops. Come across as empathetic in an interaction, and you will get someone to open up more than when you are accusatory and cold.

- Surprise them. A deceptive person will always try to anticipate your questions to ensure that their replies sound natural and instinctive. A deceptive person may even practice replying to particular questions ahead of time. Try and ask them something that they do not expect, and for sure, they will stumble.

- Learn to listen more than you speak. Liars will tend to speak more compared to truthful people in an attempt to sound legitimate and win over the target audience. Liars will use a more complex sentence to hide the facts.

You should be wary of the following:
- Repetitive clearing of the throat and coughing are signs of tension.
- People who are so stressed tend to talk louder.
- When a person crack in their natural tone of voice often occurs at the point of deception.
- Stressed people often speak faster.

This is not to assume that an interaction with your partner who does the above is lying to you. But if you witness the above behavior, please proceed with caution.

- Pay attention to behavior change. A subtle alteration in someone's character can be a strong sign of deception.

You should be careful if a person:
- Keeps using extreme, exaggerated or superlatives replies, for example, when some respond, everything is 'brilliant' or 'awesome' instead of a simple good.

▢ Answering questions using short answers, refusing to provide details.
▢ Starts speaking more formally, this is an indication that the person is getting stressed
▢ Exhibits lapses in their memory at critical times, despite the person being alert during an earlier interaction.

- Pay close attention to how the person says, "No." No is a very important word that you should observe if you suspect a person is trying to lie or mislead you.

  A person usually demonstrates deceptive habit when they:
▢ Say "no" in a singsong way
▢ Say "no" after hesitating
▢ Say "no," and they look in a different direction
▢ Say "no" that is stretched over a long period
▢ Say "no," and they close their eyes

- Asking follow-up questions. No one would ever wish to be lied to. But it is very vital to remember that people get uneasy with particular questions because of personal embarrassment or they are very dependent on the consequence of the interaction.

  If you are puzzled by a reply, explore with follow up questions. If you are in doubt, continue to ask discerning questions. In time, you will be able to spot a secret like a master.

- You should be aware of the very many compliments. Do not misunderstand me; there are sincerely nice people in the universe. But you should also watch out for people who try very hard to make a good impression.

  Consenting to all your views, constantly offering praise and laughing at all the joke you make are indications of a person who lacks sincerity and authenticity.

- Ask for the story backward. Sincere people will tend to add details and remember more truths as they repeat their experience. On the contrary, Liars memorize their story and try as much as possible to keep them similar. When you suspect that a person is deceptive, ask them to recall events backward rather than forward in time.

  For example, begin at the ultimate of the story and ask them to explain the events right before that point and then, before that and so on.

  You will notice that for truthful people, it will be easier for them to recall. Liars will often simplify the events to avoid contradicting statements.

Chapter 5: Destroying Perception and Building Understanding

Whether you are an anxious individual who is worried about how others will perceive you, or you're someone who would like to do damage control after you made a bad first impression. You should know that it is very much possible to turn the table and adjust everyone's view of you. This may sound not possible at first, particularly when you feel as if you have already made a negative impact. Trust me when I say that there are many little ways that you can show more self-confidence and appear more self-assured than before, and hence ensure that you project an image to the universe.

They say that it took seven positive impressions to mend a first bad impression.

Here are some tips that you may read on and understand some ways to feel comfortable, give off positive vibes, and change how you are perceived:

- Give off kinder vibes. While you do not have to walk around with a smile - if that is not your thing, know that there are other positive ways that you can throw off kind vibes. Your eyes and your eyebrows are a big tool that you can play with to showcase your emotion and expressions. Try it in the mirror, and you will be surprised how your face portrays what it is that you are feeling. When you radiate kindness from your face, people will notice it.

- Ask many questions. When you are interacting in a group, or you meet someone new, concentrate on being that amazing person who asks many great questions. Many people love sharing their experiences in life. You should stick to a simple question, and you will see people immediately begin to like you.

- You should embrace your own style. If you actually want to make a great first impression, you should slow down and take your time actually to get dressed. When you wear or dress up in something you feel great, other people will take notice. If you walk into a hall with your head held high thanks to the sparkling outfit, your self-confidence changes others' perceptions of you immediately.

- Putting those shoulders back. When the temptation to hunch is strong, you should keep in mind that poor body posture can make you appear less than confident. So you should push the shoulders back. By doing so, you will appear broader, and you will look taller. This is a powerful technique, and it conveys confidence. By following your body's lead, others will instantly respond.

- Relax the body. It may look tricky to relax when you are outside your personal element; it is vital to give it a try by slowing down, relaxing your face, and not crossing your arms. If you are physically relaxed, others will perceive that you are very comfortable with yourself.

- Go anyway. If you are trying to make a perfect impression, you should really show up. So you should put all networking events and get-togethers in your calendar and make sure that you attend them. When you decide not to attend such events, you will never have the chance to know others, and in that effect, they will also not get to know who you really are. So even if you do not feel like doing somewhere, take a risk and put yourself out there for people to know you well.

- Make healthy eye contact. It is completely normal to struggle with eye contact, particularly if you are nervous or anxious. Avoidance of eye contact clues to other people that you are not sure of self or not confident, which is not true at all. It could just be a bad habit that you have—so ensure that you practice eye contact in the mirror each morning to get used to it.

- Telling yourself that you matter. The best way to get good vibes for other people is to put them out yourself. To ensure that when you go out next, you should tell yourself that you matter a lot. You should try and perform a small pep talk for yourself before the event takes place, and recognize that your presence, body type, personality, and unique strengths are all critical. Empowerment and positive attitude will assist you to excel.

- Be your Charisma self. The comfortable you are a situation, the better. You should be your charismatic self by spinning yarns, laughing, smiling, or doing that which is most "you." Energy is contagious. When you go into a room radiating energy, others in the room will take notice, and you will have a positive spot in their minds as an outcome.

- Filling your mind with positive thoughts. Do you know that people can completely notice when you are concentrating on negative thoughts? That is why while it may be easier said than done, it is vital for you to remove that negative self-talk and try to be more positive.

- Taking up more space. When you feel shy, it is obvious for you to fold your arms, slouch, or shrink up. But for you to make a good impression, you need to take up more space. You should extend your presence. If you take up space energetically, others will see you as powerful, and you will feel powerful yourself. This can be done by you, putting your shoulders back, standing up tall or gesturing more to fill the space.

- You should decide how you would like to define yourself. Before you attend a situation that you will need to make a good impression, try filling your mind with positive words and use them to define yourself. By doing this, it assists you to concentrate on your energy; this helps you to give off those positive vibes more.

Chapter 6: How to Analyze a Person Instantly

The capability to analyze a person is on elf the most valuable skills one can possess. People that you interact with every day send you signals, and if you learn and pay attention to the signals that they send you without them knowing you will be able to analyze and read people easily.

Each person experiences similar basic human needs - relationships, recognition, regimentation, and outcome - with others having more dominance than others.

Most signals - visuals, vocal and verbal will be you when to slow down or speed up, when to concentrate on the details or when to work on building relationships.

Here at some techniques that you can use to analyze someone's personality at an instant.

- Pay close attention to a person's handwriting and text messages. When you compare the amount of negative and positive words can illustrate large changes in a person's personality. People who use more swear words than commonality words tend to be more agreeable; extroverts tend to use words with positive connotations. Conscientious bloggers will tend to use words about achievement.

- Pay attention to their smile. It is understood that people with a sincere smile are more likely to be married, be happier, stays married and they enjoy better health through their lives compared to those with smiles perceived to be fake smiles.

- Look at their sleep schedule. People with a morning type schedule will tend to be more focused and introverted. While, people with an evening type of schedule will tend to be more prepared to take risks, less likely to confirm and they have a far more creative, impulsive outlook of life.

- Note the type of music they listen to. You will realize that musical choices can predict personalities across four main categories:
  ☐ Rhythmic and energetic music, for example, hip-hop, rap, and electronica are agreeable, liberal, politically, and they are not afraid to speak their mind, and mostly they are extroverted.
  ☐ Those that love conventional and upbeat kind of music, for example, pop music, country and religious, are agreeable, but they are not open.

Extroverts are often rich, athletic, and politically conservative.

- ▢ Complex and reflective kind of music, for example, blues, jazz and classical indicate that a person is more open, above average intelligence and more emotionally stable.

- ▢ Rebellious and intense kind of music, for example, rock, heavy metal, and alternative, this suggests that the person is more open, above average intelligence and athletic.

- Left-handed. A left-handed person could be predicted by low levels of testosterone exposure, which is related to a high level of empathy. Left-handed men are often creative, generous, and empathetic. They also perform excellently when it comes to activities that need a rapid transfer of information, leadership experience, and they tend to have higher wages.

- Invited in their bedrooms. This may suggest their politics. Conservatives room tend to be more organized and structured; their rooms contain conventional decorations, for example, flags, alcohol bottles, and sports paraphernalia. On the contrary, liberal rooms contained a large number of varieties of books, art supplies, movie tickets, travel, and cultural memorabilia and music CDs.

Conclusion

This theory of personality type is that you are born with, live with it, and you will die with your personality type. The personality type will evolve and develop over time. You might choose to apply or use it differently on your experiences. But personality type will often remain the same throughout your life. By understanding the personality types fully, you can learn to appreciate your and recognize your weaknesses and appreciate your strengths, as well as those of other people around you

By accepting this about those around you and yourself can't only enhance your capability to work more successfully with your workmates, but with everyone you interact with.

Personality types help you to understand a person deeper in their personality, and it will assist you in analyzing people more easily, giving you an upper hand when you encounter them.

When you learn how to analyze people in the right way, it helps in your personality development, in the long run; personality development assists you to stand out from the rest. It plays a greater role in enhancing your communication skills. People ought to master the aspect of expressing their feelings and thoughts most appropriately.

Personality development molds you to a confident person who is much respected and appreciated wherever you set your feet. It assists you to inculcate positive values like willingness to learn, eagerness to assist others, friendly nature punctuality, and flexible attitude.

Dark Psychology

How to Protect Yourself from Manipulation Techniques and Dark Psychology, Recognize and Control Emotional Manipulation

By J. P. Edwin

form the information ultimately takes. This includes copied versions of the work both physical, digital and audio unless express consent of the Publisher is provided beforehand. Any additional rights reserved. Furthermore, the information that can be found within the pages described forthwith shall be considered both accurate and truthful when it comes to the recounting of facts. As such, any use, correct or incorrect, of the provided information will render the Publisher free of responsibility as to the actions taken outside of their direct purview. Regardless, there are zero scenarios where the original author or the Publisher can be deemed liable in any fashion for any damages or hardships that may result from any of the information discussed herein.

Additionally, the information in the following pages is intended only for informational purposes and should thus be thought of as universal. As befitting its nature, it is presented without assurance regarding its prolonged validity or interim quality. Trademarks that are mentioned are done without written consent and can in no way be considered an endorsement from the trademark holder.

Introduction

Psychological Manipulation comes in various degrees in various people with different causes in our fast-paced modern world and most of the time it goes unnoticed until after the fact. This is because manipulation tends to occur at childhood and continues to become a pattern if left unsupervised. It can be normalized in certain environments to the point where it is embedded into the subconscious. This is especially true for emotional manipulation. Emotional manipulation plays on a lot of our innate desires to help people, which gives the manipulator the best opportunity. Have you ever known someone who, regardless of the situation, always sees themselves as the victim? Perhaps too they always want your help in bailing them out of their messes, and you do it to be nice or out of feeling sorry for them. That is a prime example of emotional manipulation. This type can become especially common in a romantic situation.

Another frequent form of emotional manipulation takes the shape of a friendly facade presented at the beginning of a relationship where someone will share a lot of personal details about their life and expect you to do the same as well. This form of manipulation gets you vulnerable and puts your guard down so the manipulator can strike. This form shows up a lot in business and homeless people, where they will use manipulation to get monetary gain over you. Now as subtle as these tactics can be, there are fairly easy and effective counters to them such as making your opinion or boundaries firm and clear, setting clear boundaries, using reverse psychology/manipulative tactics. Now some techniques you'll find here in this book will sometimes be used by the manipulator. However, do not feel guilty. This is to protect yourself from unwanted problems or even people wanting to use you. The tactics covered in this book will use fact-based evidence from many different accredited places. A paper from Stanford University titled the ethics of manipulation points out that in the case of preventive measures i.e. using manipulation to prevent things like terror attacks, or harm incurred to yourself and other people. At that point, it is to a certain degree morally acceptable.

Chapter 1: What is manipulation

Manipulation is defined as a form of social influence which one would use to change the behavior and/or perception of others through deceptive and indirect techniques. That can result in an obfuscating of someone's goals or ideas. The reasons people use manipulation are spread wide and are usually for selfish purposes (feelings of superiority, a need to increase one's own gains, emotionally inept, etc.) It may be easy to think that manipulation is always an obvious and overt action that people will take but that is not the case. A recent research paper from the Journal of Social and Behavioral sciences stated the following about advertising "Advertising messages stimulate the potential customers' desires and train positive associations about the promoted product or company. This tells us that manipulation is all around us and in fact, we are manipulated every day by the news media, ad agencies, and other people. As a result of the increasing commodification of our world, the consumer's behavior has become a complex variable, and it is analyzed as a factor which influences the dynamics of the market and even its fluctuations." This should show you that manipulation is all around us and seen every day. The justification for the ad agency to manipulate you is to simply sell a product, this form of manipulation is the least damaging as both parties actually win in this case as first of the company makes a sale and secondly, the purchaser has bought something they are pleased with. Not all manipulation is as mild as this. The most common type is much more insidious. Let's take the following scenario, for example, you and a group of friends are hanging around the mall, enjoying yourselves. A friend makes an ill-mannered joke at your cousin's expense. She has done this plenty of times before and you have even talked to her about it. You say "Don't joke like that, it is way too early". She responds with "Chill out, just a joke". This is one of the responses she has whenever anyone speaks up against her seemingly cruel jokes. This in itself is abusive and manipulative because it devalues your emotional opinion and your own well-being in the place of hers.

With a keen eye, you can spot when the person is trying to manipulate you in conversation. In addition, there are subtle body language cues that speak more than words. Eye rolling or sighing show they're not approving of what they hear, giving you a sense of guilt over the fact that you would be bold enough to call them out on their distasteful behavior. Now that you know how to recognize manipulation it is time to learn what steps to take from here. Now dealing with manipulation can sometimes be a strange affair as the responses from individuals can somewhat very. Especially when it comes to the more common forms of emotional manipulation such as gaslighting. Which is a common theme in the majority of abusive relationships where one partner will be dominating and controlling the other one? The possible cause and lead up to this type is known as gaslighting. Gaslighting is when someone manipulates the other into questioning their own judgment. An example of this is when the husband is with his mistress and his wife catches a glance of them. Later that night she confronts him about her and he tells her she was his cousin. He proceeds to look offended and tells her how rude she is. This is one out of a plethora of gaslighting and a continuation of this manipulation could lead to devastating consequences, such as breakdowns or paranoia and in a few extreme cases even suicide. This can even be hidden as something as innocent as making jokes at your expense then denying responsibility. To counter gaslighting, for example, one should try to keep a meticulous chronology of events with documented proof as to allow them to be able to fundamentally prove the manipulator wrong. This helps to tear down the manipulator by making it easier to expose them in public. Something manipulators fear. Now like the aforementioned example when someone does rude or dishonest things to you and then tries to play it off as simple humor your best bet is to remain firm in your conviction that it was inappropriate. No matter how much they try to convince you otherwise. Keeping firm boundaries, in fact, is one of the most important ways to defend and prevent against being the target or victim of a manipulative attack. In some scenarios, it may, in fact, be impossible to utilize these tactics to help defend yourself and in such a case it may, in fact, be best for you to pull out of the situation altogether. This kind of situation is much more likely to occur in relation to a romantic relationship than it is a day to day friendship. As when individuals are in romantic relationships it is not uncommon for a partner with manipulative tendencies to think that it is okay to manipulate their partner, solely because they are their partner. In these cases, the manipulator is less likely to respond well to these generalized tactics and may, in fact, increase their manipulative attacks. If this is the case breaking away and realizing that the problem is only going to get worse will help protect you from disastrous outcomes. The easiest way to break away from a manipulator is to remember you must be adamant about keeping your boundaries firm. This means you must be prepared for continued attacks and attempts by the manipulator to get you to do what they want. Now the things covered in this chapter are only a brief overview to help you get on board and understand what manipulation is and what it looks like. From here the next step is going to be learning how to use some of the manipulators own weapons against them and to your own advantage. Before diving into different tactics of manipulation and what to do to counter them, please remember this; in some cases, the person themselves don't know they were manipulating you and perhaps we're doing it out of emotions instead of ill-will. If this ever happens, have an honest talk with the person and tell them what they did and how you feel while also explaining your reason clear and cohesive. Most will understand but the few that don't, and continue to abuse you emotionally psychologically and possibly physically, make use of the counter tactics in the following chapter.

Chapter 2: Types of manipulation and safeguards against them.

There are many different forms of manipulation you are going to encounter in your life. These forms of manipulation can cover a wide variety of bases from manipulating you from an economic standpoint, emotionally, physically. Manipulation is all around us, but it is if we recognize it that matters. Recognizing manipulation can seem to be a difficult task but it is not as hard as it seems on the surface. The reason for this is that most manipulation is relatively simple in how it manipulates emotion. It changes the basic things of social interaction such as not putting people in strange positions, making people do unreasonable things, lying to get what you want. The point being is that manipulation at its core is simply a violation of the unspoken social contract we all follow. And can be hidden in plain sight where we may or may not notice it.

To begin let's go over one of the more common methods manipulators use. Lying by omission, now that is a fairly common phrase but what exactly does it mean. Well in simple terms lying by omission is leaving out key details of something or some event. Another term for this would be a half-truth. Take this scenario, for example, your friend calls you and asks you to pick him up from the site of a recent car accident he has been in, yet when asked how it happened, he does not tell you that he was drunk-driving and ran a stop light. Instead, he simply stated he was drinking regularly and was blindsided, voiding any responsible for said accident. This is lying by omission because by virtue of your "friend" leaving out this key information you are more likely to assist them since you don't know you are helping them run from the scene of the crime. Now while this method of manipulation is pretty common it is also pretty easy to defend yourself against.

Simply put when someone puts you in a situation where they want you to make a very abrupt decision, perhaps consider the context before you decide on what you are going to do. This act of forcing you to make a decision with little background information and in a quick time is another form of emotional manipulation. By forcing you to make a choice with little information and in a short brief period the manipulator forces your hand to play too many cards at once, I.E balancing helping a friend with normal moral obligations, along with potential danger to yourself. As said prior when asked to do something take a step back to analyze the context of the situation and what you are being asked to do, and how it follows into the future? Thinking of the consequences from acts you are being asked to carry out will defend you from these kinds of manipulative attempts. Another counter to this manipulation is to spot when there is hesitation when asked of the events. If they are unwilling to give a quick cohesive answer, then they're trying to use you.

In other situations, you may encounter people who have a hard time accepting responsibility for their actions. These kinds of individuals will attempt to avoid blame and it will usually come in the form of someone trying to make you a scapegoat, or convincing you of the unjustness of a certain scenario. One example would be when a sister can't get the cookies because she is short while the brother is able to because of his height advantage. When angered by this, she'll put the blame on him by stating "I couldn't get the cookies because he's tall!". Another example would be a boyfriend is worried about his girlfriend with her friends. She claims it's because they talk about her behind her back, generalizing them. This makes the group at fault rather than figuring out if it is herself. To counter any kind of scapegoating, firstly, know your worth and your place in the situation, this is important because it is a critical component of standing your ground. And if you had no ill intention then you holding your ground is just and they're merely taking their frustration out on you. Secondly, place boundaries and make them firm and clear. This will make your limits known and there will be no refuting to it. Keep in mind, some may try and test your boundaries however you cannot give in even for an exception. This will only enable them to continue their behavior.

Although scapegoating can be seen as projection, it is more geared towards thwarting one from being blamed with projection and more geared towards shifting feelings on another. Projection is the act of placing one's own thoughts, motives, and insecurities into another person. This makes it seem as though that person is causing or feeling this way and helps relieve one of those said feelings. It can be caused by someone emotionally not liking features about themselves and verbally expel it. An example: a man beats his son whenever he gets upset and becomes highly aggressive. At one point the mother takes the son away and the father never sees him again. He continues to get angry whenever someone scoffs at him, he proceeds to call them hotheads and say that he does not get agitated so quickly".

To protect yourself from any type of projection, tell the person clearly that you are not feeling what they have accused you of and ask if they have been feeling like that recently. If it is more evidence that they have been displaying these repressed emotions or thoughts, point out directly that they are projecting onto you. Finally, remember to point out that they have no way of knowing what emotions you are feeling at the present moment.

This next technique is commonly used at stores or malls by a salesperson. It is when the person gives you a light ultimatum however gives you little or no time for you to decide. By doing this, they apply pressure on you hoping to get you to "crack" or cave into their demands. Someone who is indecisive or doesn't care that much would simply say yes.

The simple and effective method to this is to say no. if they spring it on you out of nowhere, you are not obligated to serve them. Tell them you have other things to attend to and cannot do them the task.

Amongst groups of family, friends, or co-workers, we all have a habit to tease those closest to us. While humor can be a way in which we bond with others, there is a fine line between light-hearted teasing and full-blown bullying. bullying is when we make fun of or mock someone's misfortune at their expense. Some people like to use this as a method of manipulation but others could not perhaps know that they are hurting those they think are joking along. This can create tension between a group which is never good and lead to other negative outcomes.

The best approach to take here is to discuss with the person making the joke how it makes you feel and that you do not like it or the way/tone they said it. This also allows you to gauge their intentions. If they say "oh sorry, it was only a joke" and it is the first time they said it, don't freak out. Tell them it was inappropriate or insensitive and you wouldn't rather they not do it again. Nevertheless, if they continue this behavior than perhaps it may be best to leave them as a friend. Behavior like this only gets worse from here. Additionally, it allows them to set precedent in their head that this behavior is okay, Even though you told them otherwise. From this, you can conclude that they do not see you as a true friend. for if you were, they would respect your wishes and not mock you. As painful as it is cutting these kinds of toxic people out of your life may be for the best.

Throughout our lives, we have to criticize and be criticized to improve any parts of our daily routine that need fixing. It is also needed for any team if they want to reach their goals effectively. In spite of this, harsh criticism can be unintentionally destructive and if left unchecked, it could lead to severe judgment. Usually what people want is constructive criticism, that is criticism that can help someone amend an error in their project or planning, not destructive criticism, which is used to harm someone and break someone's reputation, self-esteem and/or someone's creation. People who use destructive criticism as opposed to constructive criticism will most of the time try to keep you in control and discourage you from ever utilizing your potential to its fullest force.

For instance, imagine you're an architect and you are working on a new model for a house. Your manager gives you the rough blueprint, which you noticed there are a few areas that could use some improvements. You being sketching your own blueprint version and proceed to make a cardboard model of what they envisioned. A week later, your manager comes to see your progress, to which her face shows frustration. Raising her voice, she points out the different design from hers, comments on how the rooms look too small and talk about how the deadline is in two weeks.

Situations like these, where you are bombarded with criticism, figure out if what they're saying is constructive or destructive. Whichever one you decide it is, you want the person to get all their criticism out before trying to amend what you have done, since they will most likely ignore you while in such a state. Quietly take their words and wait until they're finished. Afterward, explain whatever changes you made and your reasons for doing such a thing. It is always good to know before being confronted if the change was worth it or not, so make sure to evaluate all your decisions. In any case, ask her to clarify her opinion. There is a good chance she will explain what she meant. However, if she were to dismiss your explanations and continue criticizing, at that point you can safely take her words for a grain of salt. And realize that they may in fact not be reflective of what is truly going on in the situation. And instead, consider that what she is saying may simply be an attempt to manipulate you and get you to do something she wants.

The silent treatment is quite commonly seen everywhere, from movies to books to even our relations with people in life. Whenever this occurs, people tend to get upset and give themselves space to think or process what they just heard/witness. On the contrary, those who want to have the upper hand will do the silent treatment so you can be concerned about them. What this achieves is since you are, in a way, striving for their attention, they will use that to hold your interest and keep you in their control. To illustrate, let's say two friends are in an argument and person A went away for days something that leaves person B to worry for days. Only now and then does person A respond briefly, only making person B seeking them out more.

First, don't consistently pursue them in any way. On the off-chance that person is mad, let them blow off steam and they'll come around in a couple of days. If not, then whenever you happen to cross paths, act as if nothing has happened. This doesn't mean give them the treatment back, but instead through your actions act simply unfazed by it.

Second, after some time has passed, send them a simple message or talk to them briefly. It doesn't need to be a long or elaborated explanation, short and to-the-point is more effective. If they don't speak or consider what you've said or given you eye contact, there is a good chance they're really trying to get control of you, to which the best course of action is to leave them be entirely. This can be difficult if it's someone dear to you, yet if they are not willing to talk to you or even compromise, it is not worth the time and effort in the long run.

Victimizing, or playing the victim is an extremely familiar type of manipulation. It is one form of manipulation that can be prevented or amplified at childhood. Any incident or accident where a child is a perpetrator usually will not end with the child seeing themselves at fault for what they have done. This is because a child has a very simplistic understanding of the world around them. But because of this, it is also easy for a parent to help or hinder the development of this behavior.

So what is victimization exactly? In simple terms, victimization is when someone is always acting like they are the victim regardless of whatever situation they are in. This behavior is rooted in childhood where if a child acts like they are injured and the victim of something negative happening to them from an external force than usually their parents will come to help save them. This can lead to negative conditioning where someone never takes responsibility in a situation and begins to start seeing themselves as the victim. A good example of this kind of behavior would be in a setting where two parties are driving and the person driving is currently holding on to their passengers' wallet for whatever reason and is then subsequently requested by the passenger to give them their wallet but doesn't because of their driving. From here the passenger begins to start grabbing for the wallet from the driver. As this is going on the driver ends up inevitably crashing because of interference from the passenger. And then in this situation, the passenger says it's all the driver's fault for this.

Another example of this kind of behavior would be where executive sender gets a response that the recipient didn't get his delivery on time and blames the shipping department. Without her realizing it, she did not ask the department if they were able to meet the deadline. These examples under more scrutiny reveal the real issue with always playing the victim. And that is that when someone always plays the victim they are unwilling to take responsibility. This feeds into manipulation because we as humans have a tendency to want to always help someone when they are in a victimized situation. Countering the manipulation of someone who always plays the victim can be difficult because of how it feeds on our innate desire to help other individuals. But the fact is it is simple to spot when someone is simply playing the victim by their response to you calling them out. What I mean by this is that if someone is clearly in the wrong when it comes to a certain situation, and they continue to keep protesting and protesting that they are innocent and not the victim. Then they are most likely attempting to manipulate you. This can best be countered by first acknowledging when someone is playing the victim. And then from their bringing this behavior up to them and explaining why it is bad and how it hurts you.

The last form of manipulation I will be covering in this chapter is also the most destructive and that is intimidation. Intimidation at its most basic level is instilling the fear of retaliation into someone in the hopes they will do your bidding. At its core, this can mean threats of physical violence, Threats of withholding something of value from someone. Intimidation is often used in romantic relationships where one partner will use or threaten violence to another partner to get them to do what they want. This form of manipulation is perhaps the most dangerous because of the element of physicality attached to it which is where most intimidation comes from. Take this scenario, for example, Angelina and Brad are dating for a period of about six months. At some point, Angelina decides that she wants to go out with her girlfriends shopping at the mall. Brad says no you can't go I don't trust you. Angelina insists that she will go out regardless of what Brad says. From here Brad says "Well I'll beat you if you go anyway." This is a prime example of intimidation as a manipulation tactic. Basically, any time in which a person threatens you in any way if you do not do what they ask of you can be considered a form of intimidation. This sadly can be hard to always defend yourself from the best thing to look out for before entering any type of relationship with someone is if they have a short fuse or any type of anger issues. If in a relationship someone begins to exhibit this habit of constantly always playing the victim then there is usually no saving them or opportunity for them to change. As this type of behavior tends to be rooted in narcissism something that is damn near possible for someone to change. But intimidation does not always mean violence it can also take the form of someone threatening to withhold something from you if you do not follow through with their demands. Take this, for example, you and your girlfriend are having a heated argument and your girlfriend threatens to not let you leave the house or she will break up and leave you. This is emotional intimidation as opposed to physical. In short, what this is, is when someone uses the threat of large emotional consequences as motivation to try and get you to do something they want. This form of intimidation is not always as black and white as mentioned in the example prior. Often times, in fact, it can take the place of unrealistic requests or ultimatums. These tend to be as simple as you must do whatever I ask of you and any disagreement with me will be seen as an insult to my person. This kind of attitude in anyone is toxic and dangerous and must be avoided at any cost. That is, in fact, the best way to cope with this type of manipulation. Simply break it off as the type of individual who uses intimidation is not likely to be the type of individual to change the course of their behavior very quickly. And remember Intimidation can take many different forms from aggressive body language to threats of physical violence. Plainly put a being demanded to do something due to the risk of consequences is intimidation. And something that you should avoid at any cost. Now that you have gained an idea of the types of and methods of manipulation hopefully you now know how to avoid them and what to look for in relationships going forward into the future. In concluding the number one safeguard you can take against any form of manipulation is firmly standing your ground and ensuring that the boundaries you set are respected and crystal clear for the other party to understand.

Chapter 3: Personality Disorders and manipulation.

Many individuals who display manipulative behavior, in some cases, have personality disorders that make them more inclined to engage in manipulative behavior. It's hard to who can have what, especially these potential people are people you grew up with or known your whole life. However, it can grow and be hardened to their subconscious, where they act on it without even giving it thought. When these disorders cloud their way of thinking, they can sometimes almost take on a new personality. For instance, while in a normal situation a person would be usually willing to admit responsibility for their actions. For a borderline, in this case, they would put the blame on others and guilt-trip them into thinking so. For example, an individual with Narcissistic Personality Disorder might go out of their way to try to and skew a situation to make them look innocent, emotional manipulation is the main way these kinds of people achieve this goal. The problem with people like this is identifying the symptomology of these disorders and who is likely to have them. Because as a result of their psychopathologies they have become experts at masking their symptoms, as a result, it can be a very tricky task as one could easily presume someone is a narcissistic simply because they are utilizing faulty information to come to this conclusion. This along with the fact that many personality disorders share overlap with other conditions that affect both the body and the mind adds to this difficulty. As a consequence of this, it makes more sense to focus on the characteristics rather than the direct symptomology. Beginning with one of the most common types of personality disorder Narcissistic Personality Disorder (NPD). People afflicted with NPD tend to exhibit some of the following key behaviors according to the Diagnostic and Statistical Manual of Mental Disorders

A Grandiose sense of self-importance, meaning that their sense of self-worth is highly inflated and as a result, they may view the actions they take as somehow better than everyone else. This is one of the ways in which a narcissist can justify their own terrible behavior, i.e. since I'm better than everyone else I can do as I please toward them

A need for excessive admiration, this is characterized by an intense desire and want to belong and have their achievements and person praised. This can manifest in the form of emotional manipulation. Via the Narcissist tearing down another individuals accomplishments and works. These are all the symptoms which the narcissist carries within them and what makes them so vicious

The two other major aspects of NPD are a sense of entitlement to special treatment. This tends to take the form of unrealistic demands and request that can end up placing an individual in a compromising or unfair spot. This can provide a lot of fuel for mental manipulation by the narcissist trying to play the victim to get you their target to give in and do what they ask of you. While also exhibiting the aforementioned behaviors pretty much all narcissists can be characterized by an overt lack of empathy.

Meaning that they will have no issue using you for something and then subsequently leaving you out to dry. As a result of this probably their most dangerous behaviors as it can allow them to justify all sorts of things in their head. Avoiding narcissists can be a difficult task but it is possible to look out for repeated patterns of the aforementioned behavior. The way they will try and manipulate you is by them almost always playing the victim and then trying to get you to second guess yourself. Your best defense against a narcissist is to honestly just leave the relationship when it becomes too much. There is no fixing them, there is no pleasing them. They will just want more and more, that is why simple going too little to no contact with them is your best bet in avoiding their destructive manipulative tactics.

Along with NPD, there is another lesser known personality disorder called BPD. Borderline Personality Disorder BPD or Emotional Unstable Personality Disorder is a pattern of abnormal behavior that is indicated by an unstable sense of self. This unstable sense of self tends to manifest itself in an ever-changing view and opinion of who they are, their self-worth and what their goals are in life. Where the problems with self-image come from, it's that they do not have an identity they can see themselves as, due to the changing emotions and desires constantly. As well as an instability their emotions and relationship with others, accompanied by feelings of emptiness or abandonment. These feelings of abandonment and emptiness can many times be self-sabotaging and lead to the individual damaging themselves when their goal the whole time was to protect themselves. In a sense, the individual who is afflicted with a borderline personality disorder does not know who they are or what they want. And as a result of this unstable and rapidly changing behavior things can quickly ramp up to a state where manipulation comes into play, and on a destructive level at that. This can be were unintentional manipulation can come from. It should be noted too that this emotional instability tends to be characterized by many peaks in valleys in their emotions and behaviors sometimes lasting for days to weeks at a time.

Now while borderlines will emotionally manipulate others, it is not intentional rather it is done because of various factors from neurobiological to childhood trauma to environmental factors. These behaviors are used as a defense mechanism to prevent them from incurring further trauma upon themselves. And not as a malevolent thing. You have a couple more options in dealing with a borderline than you do someone who is a narcissist or sociopath. In some cases, you may even be able to communicate to the borderline individual their behavior and how it is damaging and unintentionally manipulative. If they do not respond well to this kind of intervention, run and leave as your life depends on it. Borderlines can become extremely destructive very easily. At different times, borderlines can feel an array of emotions, with much greater ease and depth than the average person. When they experience happiness or joy, it will be exceptionally high most of the time. On the contrary, this will lead to them feeling profoundly low whenever they feel depressed, guilty, angry or angst. This can cause them to harm themselves, through self-mutilation or decorative behaviors. This plays into how a borderline will manipulate you on an emotional level. Remembering this will serve you well. Now there's one more personality disorder that you should be on the lookout for. And that is Antisocial Personality disorder or APD. APD is better known to the public as psychopathy or sociopathy, now this designation of psychopath or sociopathy does not mean that all individuals with ASPD are out to kill you. No, it's actually quite the contrary people with ASPD tend to be characterized by a repeated pattern of disregard for the boundaries and respect for others. As a result, they can be very, very good at manipulating someone into doing what they want. The big thing to look for is the superficial charm or glib, as most sociopaths are very excellent at putting on a mask. In simple terms, this means that they will try to tell you what they think you want to hear and as a result can very easily suck you in with their fake charm. This thought is how you can easily identify them. If you're talking to someone and your gut instinct feels that they seem disingenuous or they are trying to put on a front, then go with that gut instinct it exists for a reason and will help you. Your best bet in trying to avoid their manipulation tactics is to very subtly call them out. What this means is if someone is trying to talk you into something and it seems off to tell them "no you're trying too hard". When they are trying too hard is really the telltale signs of sociopathic manipulation as these people get bored very easily so when they think they have found a new target for their manipulation they will try everything in the book to get that target to do what they want.

Chapter 4: Success and Manipulation

So far in the book, we have covered the various types of manipulation, the kind of certain individuals who would repeatedly, and sometimes consciously, do this behavior and how to counter them for protection. You may have gotten the impression that any or all manipulation is harmful, not worth the damage of any kind and should be avoided at all times. That is a tough front to break down, especially since not many, but plenty of, common figures are used as examples of said behavior. Rightfully so, as it has harmed millions of people. That is not always the cause as this chapter will surely show you that this can be used for greatness for one's self and, at most, be used as a tool for utilitarianism. Throughout time and human history, there are numerous examples of the world's most cunning leaders and the most infamous rulers, known and unknown, who have shown that manipulation for the people and nation is a greater gain than for one's self. It is never an easy path for these kinds of people, but the rewards are tremendous and it will have rippling effects. The outcomes of these tactics, used with care, have created prosperous civilizations and brought innovations and machinery we still use and marvel over today. This shows that when used for good, manipulation can give one prosperous wealth and large amounts of power all for the greater good. On the other hand, when these skills are misused and utilized by those with an overly ambitious mind and malicious intent, the resulting consequences have caused the genocides of million and have led to the creation of men with armies with an unstoppable force at their disposal. Because of some of the negative connotations associated with these things, the stigma will no doubt arise yet some of it can be untrue. We will go over the benefits of benevolent manipulation and the success of it and how you can use it to help benefit you and perhaps use it to even try to help other people. They made even like you more amongst the prominent figures, Julius Caesar is one who was able to use his manipulation to become a dictator and do good by his lower-working people of Rome. Little is known about his childhood but we knew he first started his career in the military, making a great name for himself because of the enemies he defeated and battles won. His greatest achievement in the military was the invasion of the galleries, which he knew there was internal tensions in the tribes and took advantage of them. This also helped him in the political aspect of Rome because of all the strategizing he did in the field. He progressed through all of the ranks in almost a decade, until he became consul of the

Roman republic, the highest political office. Once he was in office, many changes came about. One of them was the integration of those who lived outside of Rome. Since they weren't born in Italy, they were not granted full citizenship, which also restricts their rights. Caesar gave them full citizenship and they were able to contribute to society. During his dictatorship, there were numerous families with 2 or 3 kids who were not working and living in poor conditions. Caesar distributed jobs to the families and also allowed pieces of land to them, some of them even working as Freeman for landowners. He also cleared a whole year of debt for low to moderate dwellers, giving them relief. It is unfortunate that his assassination came to fruition by those closest to him. The main reason behind the betrayal is because the Senate disagreed with Caesar's political campaign, in spite of the good it has done for the republic. Caesar himself wasn't fond the title of "king", but that did not persuade the betrayers from executing their plan. On the ides of March, Caesar was lead to his demise as his friends stabbed him 23 times, leaving him to die from blood loss. He was a tremendous loss to Rome and history and shows an example of how power can make those around envious.

Many tragic examples such as Caesar have been told before and there are many others that are the opposite. Long after it's time and likely the most prominent example in manipulation history would be Niccolò Machiavelli and his renowned book *the Prince*. If his name sounds familiar, then you may have heard of Machiavellianism, a political theory based off of him that views any means can be used if its intent is to maintain power. This central crux of the Prince has formed the basis of many modern political doctrines such as Realpolitik the idea in politics of removing morals and fake ideologies and removing all other preconceived notions from a political argument or debate. *The Prince* touches on ways to manipulate politicians and organizations through means of military, persuading powerful figures and making those who are soldiers to you fear you by means of how you conduct yourself. For instance, if one were to come across an evil man, he should not show any good to him for it will do him harm in the end. What this means is that in a room full of liars, what sense or good does it do to be morally good? By always telling the truth, you can never be on the advantage and your opponents will always plan ahead because of your cards. In this situation, where you are a high authority in a city, you must always be ruthless in your dealings with others. Never give a benefit of the doubt and never show mercy.

Another instance, Niccolò proclaims that lying and deceit should always be at one's disposal and home if needed. Always look as if you are truthful and forgiving, and people around you will see you as benevolent. In spite of this, those who are particularly immoral, who you also deal with, one should always be ready to cheat. A person should have the appearance of, let alone actually being, virtues so that one can have the least amount of suspicion. Nevertheless, he should always be ready to cheat or lie, to gain the upper hand to his contemporaries.

Even to this day, whenever *the prince* gets brought up, it brings both praises for how timeless and innovative it was in the 16th century and controversies for how ruthless and heartless the contents described. Like *the 48 laws of power*, people have criticized it for the lack of humanity and encouragement of ruthless behavior. It also doesn't help its case when most of the readers of these books are criminal, both in jail/prison and out. Of course the book cannot be utilized at its fullest for an average citizen, however, there are plenty of truths in the book that can help one maneuver in a workplace. As Niccolò makes clear, if someone is out to do you harm, it would be in your best interest to cheat them to protect yourself and your team.

Like many instruments, either created or founded, by humanity are amoral in essence. They alone cannot do evil nor good to others, it is all dependent on the user. This applies just as much to manipulation for there are many examples of great figures rising to the top or inspiring others, such as Martin Luther King Jr and Adolf Hitler. It may not be well known in the current year, but these two men share many common traits of thinking and manipulation yet only one has been deemed as the most despicable person in all the history books. The reason these two are being brought up as examples is that they contrast very greatly from their backgrounds, ethnicities, where their problems lie, and what they did as rising figures of their respective nations. It will also help you to understand just how influential one can be and how one can be just as influential to, hopefully, help others to be seen and to bring light to problems that are profoundly overlooked.

A common observation is a fact that both figures are charismatic men who had a magnetic pull that people were drawn to. For both men, their respective groups were oppressed one way or another, with Hitler's nation under poverty and reparations and MLK Jr. people abused in nearly every establishment. This would allow them to make empathic connections with their people. In the case of Hitler, he was able to connect with the heart of Germany due to how the Versailles treaty crippled the nation. When he spoke, he appealed to their hopes, fears, and deepest desires, offering salvation and redemption from those who put them in this devastating state. As you know the rest, this would pave the way to his rise as chancellor and forming the national-socialist party. The slaughter of more than 6 million people was done by the very same people who would obey and die for the führer. Even after 1945, there were hunts for the remaining Nazi who was hardcore.

At the same time, it is hard to deny the striking similarities to Martin Luther King Jr's upbringing. Far before he was born, black Americans have suffered a long history of oppression in the forms of slavery and violent racism, such as lynching, cross-burnings, blatant discrimination, etc. By the time MLK Jr was born, he could have easily been jaded or cynical towards his oppressors and call for the genocide of all white Americans, however, he didn't. Instead, he pursued education and took an interest in politics from his schools and public organizations. He was a top student at his college and graduated with many degrees. With all the debating knowledge and skills he acquired, he took an active stand against oppression not just in the Montgomery bus boycott, but in his speeches as well. He spoke with articulated conviction in his voice and addressed broader issues, such as poverty and economic injustice, rather than limiting it to just racial issues. Many people of his color, church and other organizations recognized this in him and were rallying behind him in no time. It was astonishing how the people rally with him and the cause awhile protesting peaceful and demonstrating how the police are the ones to be aggressive first. MLK Jr. was a courageous speaker who was able to send powerful messages across all people. Of course, similar to Julius Caesar's fall,

MLK Jr was killed outside his motel room despite all the justice he was bringing to the people.

All in all, two men from vastly different backgrounds and with different goals have utilized the power of manipulation and historically will never be forgotten. The large groups who were behind the men were, in a sense, manipulated because Hitler and Junior appealed to their emotions and frustration. But one of them used manipulation as a tool for good, to rally against the injustice using peaceful means, while the other used it from the righteous fury he had for those who wronged him and of burning passion. Manipulation, like many things, will always be at the disposal of anyone who has a goal in mind and rigid beliefs. In business, your company can't thrive if the competition has a better profit. You'll naturally want your team to win and will try to get to the top. In social circles, there may be a toxic person who is spreading misery among others. Naturally, you'll convince your friends to help this person or kick them out. It will always be up to the person what they will do.

Chapter 5: Sales and Manipulation

When it comes to selling in business, you probably heard of the expression "you can sell anything if you have the right mind".   There is truth to that since an individual must know the techniques of persuasion of the salesperson to sell the product to the customers. There's a reason used-car salesman have the reputation that they do of being able to take any crappy used car and convince someone that it is substantially better than what one can perceive.

In spite of this practice, criticism is almost always directed towards them for the usage of manipulation. The line between persuasion and manipulation can be blurred. Especially in a business where high amounts of money and people's jobs can be at stake and as a result this line can end up being crossed so many times it can be hard to tell which is which. In this chapter, we'll clarify how salespeople use manipulation to successfully sell their product and how you can use the same tactics for your own business or for your own ventures.

Business always has the need to sustain the customer's needs first before even introducing a product. Once the product is made with that in mind, the salesperson will persuade and, in this case, manipulate you into buying. See a lot of products are designed to pray on basic human emotional instinct as a result. Most of the salesperson's tactics are rehashed or "lite" versions of previous types of manipulation and the main goal in doing so are to turn a profit. With these things in mind, let's explain how these tactics work. One example is hitting the customer with facts or statistics. A salesperson is trying to sell bike helmets for $75. The next customer he encounters, he brings up how in the last year, children between the ages of six and fourteen are more likely to get into fatal bike accidents. This makes it easier for him as this applies to the customer's empathy. Via playing on the customers' innate desire to help protect their children and ensure that no injuries befall to their child. To take it a step further, the salesperson will cut the customer a one-time deal, giving a 15% discount if he purchases it right now. This manipulation is leaving little to no time to decide. And oftentimes this claim of a 15 percent discount is in fact actually given to every potential customer encountered by the salesperson. Thus, creating the illusion that his sale is special to them only. This pressures the customers thinking it would be indisputable and almost inane to not purchase the helmet right then and there. As well as convincing the customer that this deal is immoral to not take it also plays on the fact that humans love exclusivity so if they are convinced that this deal on the bike helmet or car or whatever it is being given at a good deal only to them then they will take it. As a result of these sales tactics at the end of the day, the salesperson person has now sold something at an incredibly marked up price when in reality it values is substantially less than what it is being sold for. It should be known that they do this for positive reinforcement, making you feel good about the purchase. Remember they are trying to satisfy the customer's needs while making a profit. In a simple sense, sales and manipulation both play on simple psychology. If you ever take a look at some advertisements, you may notice how they show that the individuals who are using their products seem incredibly happy or like their life has been fulfilled simply because they are using this product. As a result of the manipulation utilized in sales, professional businesses will be very careful to avoid doing something that will give them a negative or tarnished reputation, henceforth they usually pride themselves on a quality product. With this in mind, how exactly do you avoid manipulative sales tactics? Well, that question has an answer that is fairly similar to how you avoid other manipulation tactics except the end goal is different. You need to keep to yourself so if say for example you have been smart and done your research and know that a given a car is worth perhaps twenty-five thousand dollars. And you go to a car lot and the car salesman is trying to sell it up at thirty thousand by throwing in a large number of unwanted luxury features. Then from here you need to be blunt and bold with the salesperson and tell them well "Hey buddy I know I can get this hunk of junk for 25k somewhere else". See in simple terms most car salespeople tend to hedge their bets on the fact that people will be squeamish and perhaps not stand up for them self. As a result when going to buy anything be bold and confident. This act of being bold and confident helps show the salesperson that you mean business and may perhaps be difficult if not impossible to trick. Lastly, let me briefly explain how advertising uses emotional manipulation tactics to get you to purchase their products. One of the main tricks advertising agencies like to use is something psychologists call the "Fear of missing out" what this means is say Apple releases a new iPhone and they run all these ads for it well their betting less on the advertisements selling the phone and more on a cultural phenomenon. See in basic terms if everyone you know and all the people around you begin buying up these iPhones than you yourself is going to be very tempted to buy one. Your reasoning will be mostly subconscious such as not wanting to be left out of the new loop and wanting to fit in. The other tactic ad agencies like to use is sex. We have all heard the term sex sells well this can be seen in a lot of the way things are subtly sold and the shapes they may make it adds. As a result of these things remember whenever you are watching an advertisement to pay close attention to see if it is trying to perhaps play on some of your subconscious and innate desires. This includes things like scantily clad women, suggestive shapes and figures within the ad. Now that you know how advertising plays on simple emotions you can avoid it better. The most important thing to remember when making any big purchase is to deal only in facts and logic and disregard any emotion you might have towards it. This is may or may not come as a surprise but most of the motivation that comes for a purpose is dictated by emotion rather than logic. As a result of this emotion over the logic that people use most if not all manipulative sales tactics try and play on our emotions as opposed to logic. Remember this when going to something and ignore the emotional cues. This can be difficult especially when it comes to buying a house. Real estate can be an issue where realtors will try many different tactics to try and get you to buy a house. Their main trick will be by trying to sell you on the emotional appeal of a house's aesthetics something that is not important. You can always counter these emotional claims from a realtor by firmly and strongly disagreeing and holding your boundaries firmly and clearly, in doing so you also set the precedent that you are not one that is easily susceptible to manipulative tactics. These tactics can even be seen in the supermarket in how they will sometimes show an item as being marked down even though it is not. What I mean by this is that they will advertise a product as being for sale when in reality it is not what this means is that they will always label it as being on sale even though it is not. Their goal is to trick you into thinking that by not purchasing it you are missing out on some kind of deal, when in fact it is quite the opposite this plays on the human fear of missing out on a good deal. Now that you know the tactics salespeople use you are better equipped to avoid them. On the flipside, if you are a business owner yourself you can utilize these little psychological tricks to your own advantage and in doing so hopefully acre great wealth and success for yourself. It is important to remember that these tactics are not coming from a place of maliciousness on the side of the salesperson but simply put. They use positive reinforcement to get what they want and to get you to think you want it. Therefore it is not entirely a malicious thing. With these thoughts in mind, you are now armored and prepared for whenever you set foot into the sales floor. And can hopefully utilize these tricks in your daily life to bring yourself great success.

Chapter 6: Why Manipulation?

We finally have come to the last chapter of the book and it holds a very important question. Throughout this book, we have covered many different topics regarding manipulation and what they are or could look like and how to avoid them. But the question of why people manipulate others is still being answered today, with interesting answers. To begin this subject let's look at antiquity. People have been manipulating each other, according to historical records and the earliest bibliography, since the dawn of humans. From as far back as the first Roman emperors, people have been using tricks to play on simple innate human emotions to get what they want from others. By other promising false things, or playing on primal human fears, people have attained a certain great power, via using these simple psychological tricks to their advantage. The problems begin to arise when people use these techniques start to commit immoral acts on humanity, i.e. Joseph Stalin, Adolf Hitler. Individuals like the ones mentioned prior are the types who use manipulation out of personal conviction. The same reason can be applied to benevolent people, such as Gandhi, John F Kennedy. In simple terms, this means that a strong and rigid idea or belief is one of the main drives for them to use any means necessary to accomplish it. For example, in the case of Joseph Stalin, Communism drove him to exterminate millions of people without care. Or Hitler who killed millions of minorities all in the sake of a profound belief he conjured up; "Arian purity". Hitler, for example, gained his power by taking advantage of a country that, at the time was gripped by fear and extreme economic downturn. Of course, he seized the opportunity and took these fears and said to the people "if we do not do something drastic than these things will only get worse". this was accomplished by blaming people like Jews, or Jews who were Communists. He once said, "my beloved people, we must exterminate them, for a look at the disastrous state of our country, it has been caused by these monsters".

Everyone who gave Hitler the time was enchanted by his conviction and attention-grabbing aura. This was all done subtly, of course, it was a prime example of victimization multiplied by a massive magnitude. By telling the German people that they had been extremely victimized by both the world and the allies, which while true to a certain degree, he was able to assemble a massive force of angry individuals behind him. It is a powerful tool when emotions and time are aligned right. Now shifting our focus to the modern world in modern individuals who utilize manipulation such as abusive lovers, powerful men, salespeople, and agencies. Their reasoning for doing these things is the same in the past. See modern psychology, according to Maslow, states that a human being must sustain various needs through whatever resources they can get, all to attain the highest state of function. This high state is something akin to transcendence, internal peace if you will. This is recognized as self-actualization. It is the top of Maslow's hierarchy, which is when a person realizes their own talents and potential. That alone is what will drive a person to achieve what they want or need with ease. Attaining a great worry free life is something that all people obviously and subconsciously strive for, but for some people, a missed wiring inside the human brain can lead them to take these goals much too far. By this, I mean that in the pursuit of pleasure, whether that be sexual or sadism, and wealth some people will do whatever is required to attain that goal, even if it means damaging and destroying another person in the process. Sometimes victims of this behavior tend to believe they can fix these types of people, or they themselves can change, which results in Stockholm syndrome.

Many real-life examples are because of this relationship and it can stem far back as childhood. This behavior can reach a point where it will even become self-sabotaging, leading to the individual destroying themselves in the goal of reaching something. In others, past trauma can lead to these behaviors. Take the individual who due to growing up in an environment full of abuse and violence who had to lie and be manipulative to survive for example. They may end up entering a romantic relationship and begin using manipulative tactics such as playing the victim or use intimidation to get what they want out of their partner. Out the simple virtue that it what was the kind of behavior, they saw growing up, so as a result, they have come to believe that this is the only way to do something since this kind of stuff has become so normalized to them. People who use manipulation, for this reason, are not people who can easily be helped. As their reason for using manipulation tactics is due to mental illness or past trauma, which is something that some people never recover from. Thankfully it is fairly easy to spot these kinds of individuals when you first encounter them. People who are overly needy of praise or need constant validation or who always sees himself as the victim in any situation they are in or straight up ignore you whenever they don't need you. These kinds of people have learned that manipulation can get them the feelings that they crave so badly with as minimum effort needed. As a result, ranging from things like poor parenting or experiences which validate these kinds of behaviors. As a result, they will be very unlikely to break these negative behavior habits and in fact, as a result, are more likely to continually do the same thing even if it destroys them. On the entirely opposite side of the spectrum, there are entities that utilize manipulation to gain the things that they want. News agencies, political parties, stores, salespeople, etc. Use the power of manipulation to usually further financial or power objectives that take priority first. Not too dissimilar from dictators or despots who did the same thing in the past. This kind of manipulation, while also more common, tends to also happen on a much larger scale. The way the news media or any reporting outlet, for instance, uses manipulation is by trying to only tell you what you want to hear as opposed to telling you the truth. They omit particular details about an event to invoke an emotion. This always has to be done subtly by only reporting on certain news stories or events. While the iPhone ad that may play on the same news channel will try and get you to purchase a brand new product by virtue of it seeming cool or flashy, and playing on the fact that people like things that make them feel exclusive or special while lastly getting into that innate fear of missing out on the big parade. The way a salesperson for an example will agree or reinforce any foolish or stupid preconceives notion a potential buyer may have about a car all in the desire to sell said car while in itself neither malicious nor good. It is still a tricky tactic that not many people are aware of. This blatant unawareness is what these people feed on they know that most people are unaware of the fact that they are getting ripped off or falling under the spell of a manipulation. And as a result, they are able to continue using this kind of behavior to get us to buy their products no matter our life routines or the consequences. The main thing to keep in mind when realizing all of this is that no one ever thinks they are the villain in a situation, they will always assume that they are in the right regardless of the result of their actions. And as a result when you try and show them the toxicity of how they are behaving it is highly likely that instead of in fact listening and regarding what you are saying, it will only further embolden them and push them to move on to a better target. And get them to further behavior. This is the number one problem with the manipulation that forgets. Manipulators can be experts at presenting themselves as beautiful and engaging individuals. Dualistic thought it is the same aspect that allows them to reap so much destruction their ability to glib and charm you with fake promises and threats creates a perfect storm. While for some it may be trauma, the idea of gaining power or wealth that drives them to manipulate. For the very select few, they manipulate simply because they like to hurt people and like to see pain inflicted on them. This leads to a whole new breed of manipulation, which can be called psychopathy. Psychopaths are IMMENSELY dangerous beings yet they are few in numbers today in the United States. These kinds of people are extremely hard to detect which is a large part of what leads to the difficulty in dealing with them, how you can defend against something if you do not know what you're guarding yourself against. While manipulation has been used in extremely negative ways by quite a few people. As mentioned previously it can also be used in survival situations or for your own good. With this I mean when manipulation is used in cases like negotiation or certain forms of policy making the net benefit can become better than the cost. I.E lying to an opposing county to avert a war that could lead to a large amount of death and destruction. Diplomats and ambassadors are created for this sole purpose and serve a great role for the nation. As shown in chapter 4, respected individuals have demonstrated how this tool that had the stigma of immoral intent behind it can be used for the greater good. It is warranted, in spite of the good it can do. Numerous events and things in the world always require the correct timeframe and the precise execution to successfully manipulate others. Sometimes you may be worried about how others will view you or will change the way they think about you. This may be the case, however, you can always state your purpose in doing so and hopefully, if they are a sensible person, they'll understand. If they do not, you have to wonder if it's because of a lack of understanding and not wanting to connect or they had other plans which you foiled before they can enact them. You can never know what kind of people you hang around with. Your parents may have told you time and again "don't let others get control over you". There will always be those who are natural born leaders, who are able to bring others up and help towards a common goal. On the other hand, there are people who are deceitful masters and see others as pets for their amusement and tools to increase their gains. You can never know, only anticipate. If you had the thought "what if I am able to prevent any of this from happening?", you should know there isn't a way. It's only when you can plan ahead yourself that you can prevent it. If you ever need a reference to a book, you can use this.

Made in the USA
Middletown, DE
11 March 2020